Anger Overload in Children:

A Parent's Manual

By David Gottlieb, Ph.D.

Table of Contents

Preface

What prompted me to write this parents' manual were the calls and e-mails I received from parents around the country who read the article I wrote in 2001 about "anger overload" in children. The article was written for Attention magazine, and has been picked up over the years by several popular parenting websites. I coined the phrase "anger overload" to describe the intense angry reactions some children have when they do not get to do what they want. In the article I outlined some approaches parents can use, but many people have contacted me after reading the article and have asked what exactly to do to help their children. In this manual, I have put together a number of techniques I have suggested over the years.

I have organized the strategies in a systematic way. The first task is sometimes the hardest for parents to complete. I ask parents to observe their child's tantrums and to record the sequence of behaviors that occur during the outburst. Parents sometimes struggle with this suggestion, because they want to stop the tantrums, not observe them. But before you can intervene successfully you must get a clear handle on what is going on. You will discover certain patterns about your child's angry outbursts, and then you will be able to do something about them.

Another concern that parents express early on is whether knowing some patterns will help if there are some tantrums that do not fit any pattern. It is true that there can be many different triggers and that you will not be able to anticipate all of your child's outbursts. But if you can intervene and head off anger overload even 50% of the time, you have made a huge difference in your family's life.

In the manual you will learn other tools that can help when you haven't been able to foresee an outburst. One important recommendation is to stop talking to your child when he is totally out of control. This may seem counterintuitive to parents who would like to do something to calm their child down. However, when your child is extremely overheated, it is unlikely you will be able to "talk" him down. In fact, anything you say may prolong your child's tantrum. Once your child settles down, there are a number of strategies you can implement to help diminish the frequency of outbursts in the future.

The first half of the manual explains strategies that you can implement and that do not require your child's participation, while the second half of the manual involves plans you develop with your child when he is calm. It is sometimes hard for parents and their children to sit down and calmly review the periods of anger overload. The younger and less verbal the child, the harder it will be. However, I have found that even six year olds can work on these strategies in many cases. One key is to wait until everyone is relaxed and not busy with something else before attempting the worksheets in the second half of the manual. I will explain in the manual how to present the worksheets to your children. You will do most of the hard work. (Something parents are used to doing!) You will direct the discussion with your children, and do most, if not all, of the writing for the worksheets. If you keep the discussion short (no more than five minutes) and wait until your child is not in the middle of his favorite game or activity, most children will want to do something about their tantrums. They usually wish they could control their behavior better, and are willing to try.

One question I often get from two parent families is whether one or both parents should plan the strategies and meet with their child. It is important that parents review the plans with each other, though you both don't have to do the worksheets with your child each night. The key is to be a united front when you are implementing the strategies. If your child feels that one of you is not behind the plans, then your child will not take the program as seriously. It is important therefore to be on the same page with your partner as you decide what to do. When you get to the stage where you are filling out the worksheets with your child, ideally you will take turns sitting down with your child, or sometimes both of you will sit down with your child in the evening to review the day's events. Often your family's work schedule and evening routine will dictate which parent has time to work with your child on a given night. And if nights are hectic for your family, the worksheets can be done during the morning or afternoon, so long as everyone is calm and not busy with something else.

Finally, to complete all the strategies in the manual will take several months. But remember you will begin to see changes in the first month as you implement part one of the manual. Part two will help your child gain more control of his behavior. The order for the strategies in part two is what I have found works best for most children. Read over all the strategies in part two before you begin this section of the manual. If you feel one idea will not work for your child, and you like another idea better, it is okay to focus on what you think will work best for your child. Also, for a number of the strategies, I suggest several ways to implement them, and you can decide which way would be more suitable for you and your child. In my practice, I encourage parents to be creative. You know your child and what might work better for him. In this manual, I offer you the tools that will help you and your child learn new ways to deal with anger and frustration.

Please note that I will be using the pronoun "he" to refer to individual children in this manual, but this usage does not refer to male children, but to any child, male or female. Anger overload occurs with girls as well as boys.

There are many people to thank, who helped me bring this manual to publication. First, I want to thank my wife Fawn for reading this manual several times and for giving me feedback. I also want to thank my children Seth, Lev, and Shira for their advice along the way.

Dr. Hubert Dolezal and Dr. Mohammad Ilyas wrote reviews that you can find on the back cover. Hubert Dolezal has been a colleague and a friend for many years. He has an active practice doing testing and therapy in Chicago. Mohammad Ilyas is a child and adult psychiatrist at Regional Mental Health Center in Indiana and has a private practice in Homewood, Illinois. Both Dr. Dolezal and Dr. Ilyas have given me advice about my writing. Thanks also to Risa Graff and Dr. Al Ravitz for your support over the years.

Lastly thanks to the parents who tried out the manual this last year, and to all the parents I have worked with over the last thirty years who have tried many of these strategies. All of you have influenced my thinking about how best to help children who have extremely angry outbursts. You can read more comments from parents on my blog: yourchildisdefiant.blogspot.com

Section I: What is anger overload?

Key characteristics of anger overload

Anger overload is an intense rage reaction to disappointment or frustration. Children and teenagers with anger overload react in an extremely loud or aggressive way when their plans or wishes are disregarded or interfered with by others. The reaction is quick and intense. They may scream obscenities, or verbally attack you: "I hate you," and "you are the worst parent in the world." A number of children express their rage physically by throwing things (at you or near you), or by actually hitting or kicking you, the furniture, or whatever is nearby at the time. While the most explosive verbal or physical reactions, such as saying "I hate you" or kicking something, usually only last several minutes, the emotional upset and angry remarks may go on for an hour or more.

When the children calm down, their behavior is not difficult to deal with, and these children can be kind and pleasant, just like other children who do not have episodes of rage. In other words, these children usually do not have ongoing behavior problems when they are not experiencing anger overload. While some children are more irritable and moody even when they are not full of rage, this is not the rule for most children with anger overload. When their anger is stoked, it is as if they change into another person, sort of like Hulk. (For those of you not familiar with the old movie or television series, Hulk is a scientist who turns into an aggressive green giant when he gets real angry.)

What is characteristic of many of these children is that they overreact to a perceived slight or disappointment. They often do not see why someone would not agree with what they wanted to do. They feel like their desires or requests were reasonable and were unfairly disregarded by someone else. And they react with fury. In other words, what would mildly frustrate most other children causes great disappointment or anger in these children. For example, one child we will discuss is Don, an eight-year-old boy. When his parents did not have a catch with him outside after dinner, he became angry to the point of throwing things and hitting his parents. Most children would be disappointed but not launch into a tantrum and physical aggression toward their parents.

A teenager we will use for illustration purposes in this manual, a 14-year-old named Jason, would overreact if he had to get off "Facebook" and give his sister a turn on the computer. Other situations that triggered his rage were when his brother quit playing a video game with him before the game was over, or when his parents said Jason could not invite his friends for a sleep over. He would start yelling at his mother, calling her a "bitch," and say things like he "hated" his life. Sometimes he also threw toys at his mother or at the wall, smashing the toys. Most teens would not react so violently if they could not have a sleep over, or if they had to share the computer, or if their sibling quit playing a game with them.

One issue that sometimes lay behind Jason's strong reactions was his feeling that he had to go out of his way to get peers to like him, that if he did not have a sleep over, for example, his peers would not want to be with him. Many teens worry about rejection and try hard to please their friends. However, most will not curse their parents or throw things at them if their parents tell them to stop "Facebooking" their friends and give their sibling a turn on the computer, or if their parents say their friends can come over to the house, but not sleep over.

Don's area of vulnerability was his small stature and his wanting to be as competent as his older brother. He wanted to practice having a catch with his parents so that he could show how good he was. He also got furious sometimes if he had to go to bed rather than watch a television show. He felt his parents were unfair because his older brother got to stay up and watch the show. Another day he threw a tantrum when his parents said he could not light the holiday candles. In this case, the issue was not his stature or competence. He just liked lighting the candles. However, his parents were in a rush to get out the door to a party and said "no, not now." Don exploded, and the parents had to bring him kicking and screaming to the car.

Interestingly, another time Don reacted with a tantrum was when he could not master a new activity (such as skate boarding) as quickly as he thought he should. With skate boarding, the disappointment had to do with Don's not meeting his own expectations. Though anger overload is usually triggered by a child's frustration with others, sometimes tantrums are triggered when a child is disappointed in himself.

Both Don and Jason would overreact when their area of vulnerability was in play. However, it would be an oversimplification to say that this was the only time they overreacted, or that every child with anger overload has an area of vulnerability. For example, when Jason got angry with his brother for quitting a video game, Jason's worry about peer approval was not a contributing factor. The issue of peer acceptance underlies some, but not all of Jason's angry outbursts. The more general theme is that Jason gets angry when someone in his family frustrates or disappoints him. Anger overload occurs when there is some frustration or disappointment that is difficult for the child to deal with.

You will not always be able to predict which events will frustrate your child so much that he will react with rage. Sometimes there is a pattern, or theme, that you will recognize over time, and sometimes you will be surprised. The more you keep track of your child's outbursts though, the more patterns will emerge. You will not be able to anticipate all outbursts, but you will be able to anticipate some of them.

The *key* criteria then for anger overload are that there is an extreme rage reaction to some frustration, and that the level of anger is out of proportion to the triggering event. Usually this is because the child misperceives or exaggerates in his mind the significance of the frustration or disappointment—like thinking that this is going to ruin his life, or that there is no good reason why he shouldn't be able to do something, or that he is being treated so unfairly. The child does not keep the disappointment in perspective, and the anger then builds quickly and is expressed in a very intense and socially unacceptable manner.

During the period of anger overload, the child or teen is not amenable to reason. It does not help to try at that time to explain anything. Not only will it not stop your child's anger, your child may get angrier if you talk to him during his emotional outburst. It will also not shorten his outburst if you try to impose a punishment at this time. The child is not thinking rationally at this point and is not able to slow down to think about what you are saying. If you can anticipate your child's behavior, or if you can catch it early, you may be able to re-direct your child.

How anger overload is different from other diagnoses

If your child exhibits anger overload, it does not mean your child has a mood disorder, like major depression or bipolar disorder, nor does it indicate a major behavioral disorder, like oppositional defiant disorder or conduct disorder. In mood disorders there are periods of elevated (manic) or low (depressed) mood. Children with mood disorders can sometimes experience anger overload; you see this particularly with children with bipolar disorder. However, bipolar children also cycle between mania and depression. Most children with anger overload do not have these mood problems. Furthermore, the strategies we will explain later for anger overload will not work as well for children with mood disorders unless the mood disorders are treated.

Most children with anger overload do not meet criteria for oppositional defiant disorder either, though they often exhibit oppositional behavior during an outburst. What is different is that children with anger overload are cooperative with adults most of time, whereas children with oppositional defiant disorder argue with adults more frequently. Furthermore, oppositional children do not usually explode during arguments. Oppositional defiant children can be lawyer-like in their disagreements with their parents or teachers, and if they curse, it is for effect, and not usually because they lost control.

Children with another diagnosis called conduct disorder do not generally care what rules adults make. They will do what they want, often without even discussing their plans with their parents. They do not get mad at their parents; they ignore them. There are no outbursts.

There is one other infrequently used diagnosis in DSM-IV (*Diagnostic and Statistical Manual-fourth edition*, which is the diagnostic manual used by mental health professionals) that on the surface may sound like anger overload, but is really quite different. This diagnosis is intermittent explosive disorder (IED). What is different is that for intermittent explosive disorder there are serious assaults and often destruction of property. For anger overload, there may be violent behavior, but not usually "serious assaults." In addition, anger overload includes verbal as well as physical displays of anger, not just physical violence.

For a discussion of many of these diagnoses and for a description of the behaviors these children exhibit, I refer you to other books about childhood disorders, including my book *Your Child is Defiant: Why is Nothing Working?* My book explains different diagnoses that can underlie a child's defiant behavior.

Changes in the new diagnostic manual in 2013

The upcoming diagnostic manual of the American Psychiatric Association will be known as DSM-V and is scheduled for publication in 2013. It will likely have a new diagnosis called disruptive mood dysregulation disorder (DMDD). There is a lot of overlap between this diagnosis and what I have written over the years about anger overload. As currently proposed, for a child to be classified with disruptive mood dysregulation disorder, there must be severe recurrent temper outbursts over a year's time. The outbursts can be verbal or physical and are out of proportion to the level of stress or provocation. This definition fits closely with the definition of anger overload.

What is different about the criteria for disruptive mood dysregulation disorder (DMDD) is how the child behaves in between outbursts. For DMDD, "nearly everyday, the mood…is persistently negative (irritable, angry, and/or sad)." For most children we have observed with anger overload this is not the case. Children with anger overload often have some sensitivities or insecurities that can lead to frustration and anger, but unless these sensitivities are triggered the mood of these children is not troubled, irritable, sad, or angry. Parents and teachers report that children with anger overload are friendly and not moody. This is different than what is proposed for disruptive mood dysregulation disorder.

Biological underpinnings

There has been much written in the psychological and medical literature about the areas of the brain and the kinds of neurotransmitters (brain chemicals) associated with anger. Some of the studies look at normal expressions of anger, while others consider aggression and violent behavior. In most cases adults, not children, are studied. While these studies do not look at anger overload per se and do not focus on children, we would still expect there to be some similarity in the brains of children with anger overload. (There may also be some differences as the brains of children are still developing.)

The two areas of the brain that are discussed most often in relation to anger are the amygdala, which is a part of the limbic system, and the prefrontal cortex, which is part of the outer cortical lobes of the brain. The prefrontal cortex is the area of the cortex that is in front. The limbic system, which includes the hypothalamus, hippocampus, and the amygdala, is deep inside the brain and is involved in emotions, pleasure, and appetite, among other processes critical to our lives. The prefrontal cortex is seen as the executive of the brain, which controls, or regulates, the amygdala and other limbic structures. The prefrontal cortex helps us evaluate various situations and plan an appropriate response.

When someone gets angry, both the amygdala and prefrontal cortex are stimulated and communicate with each other. One prominent theory is that when anger gets extreme, the prefrontal cortex has difficulty controlling or modulating the responses of the amygdala.

Over the years, scientists have looked more closely at these structures and related areas of the brain. The area of the prefrontal cortex that is especially involved with anger is the ventromedial section. "Ventral" means the underside or belly, and "medial" means toward the inside or middle. So the ventromedial prefrontal cortex (vmPFC) refers to the middle, underside section of the front outer layer of the brain!

Recent studies have looked at even more specific sections of the vmPFC. Some scientists have suggested that the posterior (rear) section of the vmPFC works to limit negative emotions while the anterior, or perigenual (front), section of the vmPFC appears associated with positive affect. Other scientists have compared the left vmPFC with the right vmPFC, and found there was greater blood flow in the left vmPFC when people experienced a lot of anger. With modern imaging techniques, like fMRI studies (functional magnetic resonance imaging) and PET (positron emission tomographic) scans, there will be even more specific studies of the parts of the brain that regulate anger.

Some studies have looked at the chemicals in the brain that are associated with anger. Serotonin is one neurotransmitter that has been studied a lot in the last ten years. Serotonin has been found to be one important modulator of emotional behavior, including anger. Low levels of serotonin have been found in people who exhibit more violent behavior. A study last year of serotonin in normal adults found that low levels of serotonin made communication between the amygdala and prefrontal cortex weaker. The study suggested that when serotonin transmission is low the prefrontal cortex is not able to control the feelings of anger that emanate from the amygdala. Other studies have found that medications that improve serotonin transmission help limit the expression of violence and rage in adults. The role of various chemicals in the amygdala and prefrontal cortex is going to continue to be an important area of study in the years to come and may lead to better medicines for the control of anger.

What does this tell us about anger overload in children? We can make tentative hypotheses (educated guesses) based on studies of adults, but these hypotheses need to be tested with groups of children, whose brains are still growing. Furthermore, we need to compare children who have anger overload with children who do not get extremely angry to see if there are anatomical or functional differences. It seems likely that for children with anger overload, the amygdala and prefrontal cortex are not in sync. It could be that the amygdala is overreacting and flooding the prefrontal cortex with anger chemicals so that the prefrontal cortex cannot manage the load. It is also possible that the problem lies not with the amygdala, but with the prefrontal cortex: the amygdala may be reacting normally to anger provoking situations, but the prefrontal cortex may be immature. A third possible explanation is that neither brain structure is underdeveloped, but the coordination between the brain areas is poor. Maybe the pathways between the amygdala and the prefrontal cortex are not mature (a metaphor being that there are dirt roads where paved highways are needed). Based on the adult studies that show the importance of serotonin, maybe the coordination between the areas of the brain is hampered by a deficit of serotonin.

What is hopeful is that in most cases we think that the problem for children is not structural damage but immature development. With "exercise" the brain will develop more quickly. The rest of the manual provides mental exercises to help children learn to control their anger. If children change their behavior, their brains change at the same time. All of a person's behaviors are mirrored in brain activity. If we learn new habits, our brains change to reflect those new habits.

Section II: How to change your child's behavior

Overview of interventions

Parents are key agents of change for children with anger overload because they are present when children most often have this problem. Parents have the power to intervene in ways that can really help. My manual provides a systematic approach for parents. The manual is divided into two parts. The first part focuses on steps you can take yourself without planning with your child ahead of time. There are charts that you fill out yourself or with your spouse, but not with your child. In the second part of the manual, I explain how to teach your child to recognize and modify his own anger. This part of the manual has worksheets that you do with your child.

One question I get from parents is how much time to spend on each step and which strategies to use first. I would recommend following the order laid out in this manual. It is important to complete part I of the manual before going on to part II. The strategies you implement in part I will help ease your child's anger somewhat, which will make it easier for him to learn the skills presented in part II. The second half of the manual outlines a cognitive behavioral approach to anger regulation that you will work on together with your child. It works on developing a child's awareness of his triggers and emotions, and teaches a child to look at things from a different perspective.

You are embarking on a process that takes time and will have some ups and downs along the way. There are biological and emotional reasons why your child reacts so strongly to frustration. So what you will learn in this book will not work over night. It will take months of effort on your part. But it will be worth it because you will be teaching your child a skill that will be so important in his life: how to control his anger. If he does not learn to control his temper, he could someday have problems in intimate relationships or on the job, whenever his frustration builds. Learning how to deal with frustration is an important life skill with huge ramifications for your child's future. It can be just as important as learning how to read and write. With this manual, you will learn how to be your child's "emotional teacher." You will teach the important skill of anger regulation. In the following chart, I list the techniques in the same order that they will appear in this manual:

Interventions for Anger Overload

Part I: Parents as the agent of change:

Observe patterns

Prevention: Lower your child's expectations or change the sequence

Early anger phase: Emotional distraction and calming strategies

Overload phase: Ignore or restrain?

When to use praise and consequences

Be a role model

Part II: Teaching your child new skills

First step: Review patterns and explain rationale

Second step: Develop your child's self-observations skills

Third step: Use labels together with calming strategies

Fourth step: Teach your child about other points of view

Fifth step: Use catch phrases to help your child think before reacting

Sixth step: Teach compromise technique

Part I: Parents as the agent of change

Begin by observing patterns

Before you can try to change your child's behavior, it is important to get a clear "read" on what is going on. When is your child most likely to lose it? Who is he interacting with at the time, and what is the issue? I suggest you use the following chart and record situations when your child experiences anger overload over the next two weeks. (A similar version of this chart appeared in my book: *Your child is defiant: Why is nothing working?)*

Chart 1: Recording angry interactions

Scenario 1: Date_______________

Who was the target adult? ________________

What did the child say or do? ____

____

What did the adult say or do?

____

____

What did your child say or do next?

____

____

What did the adult say or do next?

____

____

Anything happen then? ____

What was your child doing in the hour preceding the above interaction?

____

What was the target adult doing in the preceding hour?

____

Scenario 2: Date_______________

Who was the target adult? ________________

What did the child say or do? ______________________________

____

What did the adult say or do?

____

____

What did your child say or do next?

____

____

What did the adult say or do next?

____

____

Anything happen then? ______________________________

What was your child doing in the hour preceding the above interaction?

____

What was the target adult doing in the preceding hour?

____

Scenario 3: Date________________

Who was the target adult? ________________

What did the child say or do? ______________________________

____

What did the adult say or do?

____

____

What did your child say or do next?

____

____

What did the adult say or do next?

____

____

Anything happen then? ______________________________

What was your child doing in the hour preceding the above interaction?

What was the target adult doing in the preceding hour?

Stop here for 1-2 weeks and record at least three situations. If you can, record more examples, as it will help you to figure out which types of situations are more likely to trigger your child's anger. There are more blank recording sheets for chart #1 in the appendix.

After recording some occasions when your child has a meltdown over a two-week period, look over the data, and see if there are any patterns. Does he heat up with one adult more than another? Is he disappointed he cannot do something he wants to do, or does he feel slighted in some way? Does he feel something is unfair? Often anger overload occurs when a child feels like his feelings or ideas were disregarded or marginalized for no good reason. The child in this case feels he was entitled to something (e.g. video game time, a certain meal, a sleep over date) and rages when things do not go as he expected. Does this theme fit for your child's anger, or is there another theme?

In addition to determining the theme, see if you can identify some of the specific activities when your child's hurt and anger occur. Is it around free time activities, homework, bedtime, meals, or something else? If there are a couple situations that most likely trigger your child's anger, make a note of it. Knowing the pattern will give you the best opportunity to intervene earlier in the sequence in the future and possibly head off a tantrum.

We will use the word *triggers* to refer to 1) the situations or activities most likely to lead to angry outbursts and 2) the theme(s) that best describes your child's feelings or perceptions in these situations. This does not mean that you will be able to identify all of your child's triggers; however, if you can identify some of them, you will better be able to anticipate and modify your child's reactions.

Chart 2: Your child's triggers

A. List a few situations that sometimes lead to anger overload:

1.____

2.____

3. ____

B. What theme(s) describe your child's feelings before an outburst? (Circle whichever themes apply in some situations.)

1. Disappointed he did not get to do what he wanted.

2. Feeling that you were not fair.

3. Feeling slighted or ignored.

4. Other: ____

Here are charts #1 and 2 filled out for Don, age 8, and for Jason, age 14.

Charts 1 and 2 for Don, age 8

Scenario 1: Date: _______after school one day

Who was the target adult? _____Mom and Dad

What did the child say or do? _____ "Let's play ball outside" (It was 6:15 and already dark)

What did the adult say or do? _____Mom said: "It's dark and I'm still eating dinner." (Mom got home later than expected.) "Let's play another game when I'm done eating."

What did your child say or do next? _____ "Why aren't you playing?" He then threw the pillows off the couch. Next he went to the fireplace to try to turn on the gas knob.

What did the adult do next? _______Dad restrained Don.

Anything happen then? ____Don screamed, "I hate you," but calmed down in about five minutes.

What was your child doing in the hour preceding the above interaction? ____Don kicked a ball outside before dinner with his brother.

What was the target adult doing in the preceding hour? _____Dad was getting dinner ready and Mom was still at work.

Situations that sometimes trigger anger overload:

1. ____Not being able to do an activity with his parents, like having a catch after dinner
2. ____Not being able to stay up on a skateboard
3. ____Not being able to watch a movie before bedtime

What theme(s) describe your child's feelings?

1. Disappointed he did not get to do what he wanted
2. Upset when he was not as good at an activity as his older brother or neighbors

Charts 1 and 2 for Jason, age 14

Scenario 1: Date: ____one day after school____________

Who was the target adult? ___Mom

What did your child say or do? ________ Jason and younger brother were arguing, and then Jason began chasing his brother around the house.

What did the adult say or do? ________Mom asked Jason to go to his room.

What did your child say or do next? _______Jason began swearing at his mother: "F*** you bitch."

What did the adult say or do next? __________ "Get to your room."

Anything happen then? _______ Jason said: "No bitch. Leave me alone." He continued cursing. Mom went to the kitchen. Jason's swearing continued on and off for about a half hour.

What was your child doing in the hour preceding the above interaction? ______Jason was playing video games with his brother.

What was the target adult doing in the preceding hour? _____ Mom was making dinner. Dad was not home yet.

Situations that sometimes trigger anger overload:

1. _____ Playing competitive games with his brother
2. _____ Giving his sister a turn on the computer
3. _____ Not being allowed to have a sleep over

What theme(s) describe your child's feelings?

1. Disappointed he did not get to do what he wanted or expected
2. Feeling his parents were not being fair
3. Wanting his peers to like him

Prevention: Lower your child's expectations or change the sequence

Lower your child's expectations

Once you have an idea of the triggers for your child, you can sometimes predict when an outburst may occur. Take a look above at charts #1 and 2 for Don and Jason. In the first of our two case examples, the younger child Don typically blew up when he expected to do something and then was not able to do so. In one situation, the problem was that he thought he was going to be able to continue to play outside, but it was already dark out. The parents suggested an alternative, but Don refused and escalated. This pattern occurred at other times when Don thought he would be able to do something fun, but ended up having to wait (or not do it) because of the time of day or because other family matters took precedence. Don was egocentric and only saw that he was being denied. The parents knew then that when Don was expecting an activity after school or on the weekends, they needed to prepare him in advance that it might not happen exactly when Don expected.

Whenever the parents sensed that Don was excited about an upcoming activity, they began to use words like "maybe we will do it then and maybe we will do it the next day. I'm not sure yet" or "we have ______ to do tonight so we will probably have to wait a day or two." It was better for Don *not* to expect something and then be pleasantly surprised that there was time to do what he wanted.

For Jason, the 14 year old, one problem started when there was a disagreement with his younger brother over a video game. The boys got quite competitive during their games, and sometimes the younger brother wanted to quit, which enraged Jason. He started chasing his brother, at which point the mother intervened. She asked Jason to go to his room. He refused and began swearing. The mother initially moved toward him with the idea that he would move away and go to his room. But Jason held his ground and continued to call his Mom all kinds of names. She decided to back off (her son was bigger than she) and left the area. Jason did not follow his mother, nor did he go to his room, but kept up his diatribe in the family room for a half hour. In this case, Jason later said he felt it was unfair for the brother to quit the game when he was losing, and also felt it was unfair for the mother to tell him to go to his room when the brother started the problem, in his view.

Jason was big on "fairness," however his idea of fairness only took into account his point of view. Also Jason was particularly jealous of his younger brother. He felt the younger brother had more friends and did better in school academically as well. Parents eventually learned to predict that Jason could get angry when playing a competitive game with his brother. They limited these activities to when there were neighbor kids or his school friends over at the house (as Jason did not act this way in front of peers because he so much wanted their approval) or when a parent was in the room to help supervise the game.

Jason worried whether his peers would like him, and two other situations when he had outbursts had to do with his feeling that his parents were making it difficult for him to make friends. He sometimes erupted when his mother asked him to get off "Facebook" to give his younger sister a turn on the computer. Another situation that triggered his rage was when his parents did not want him to have a sleep over with half a dozen friends at one time. Jason did not understand his parents' concern that the boys would make noise a good part of the night and interfere with the family having a restful sleep. Jason felt his parents were not being fair to him. Since having a sleep over with a number of friends at the same time was a big issue come the weekends, the parents would either tell Jason on Thursday and Friday that there would be no sleep over this weekend or that he could have a sleep over with one or two friends (if the family did not have a lot of plans already). They also made a new rule that a sleep over with many friends at the same time would be allowed only for birthday parties. Preparing children in advance and lowering children's expectations is an important tool parents can use to prevent anger overload.

The mother of an eight-year-old girl reported to me that her child often escalated in the car after she picked her up from day care in the late afternoons. Her daughter would talk about what she wanted to do when she got home. Often what she wanted to do was play outside with her neighbor friends. This was not possible on days when the mother got off work late because the children would have little time for activities after dinner and homework. Or if the weather was bad, the mother did not want her daughter playing outside. Her daughter would start screaming if the mother said no, and this would continue even after they got home. When the mother recognized the pattern, she was able to head off an outburst by telling her daughter the evening plans right when she picked her up from day care. The child did not build up hope for playing outside that day, and did not escalate into a tantrum. For some children, the parents would need to tell their children even earlier in the day (before school) what the plans were for the evening because their children might otherwise start thinking during the school day that they would have time to play outside when they got home.

Another parent I worked with took her young children grocery shopping each week, and sometimes would get her children a little bag of candy. Though she only got them candy once in a while, one of her children reacted with extreme anger one day when he saw something he wanted and she said: "there is no treat today." The problem was that the child had come to expect candy when they went shopping, and the child did not have the ability to control his frustration. Screaming and tears began in the store and persisted for an hour after they had left. This happened again the next week when they went shopping. The mother realized the pattern, and began telling her children before they went shopping whether they would be able to have a treat that day. Predicting what would happen in the store helped this child. Another option would be to dispense with treats in the store altogether, or to go grocery shopping without the children. The idea is to avoid a child's outbursts when possible by preparing him in advance for a potentially frustrating event or by avoiding the triggering event altogether.

Alter the routine

Another child had difficulty when it was time to stop playing a video game and get ready for bed. While this could be difficult for many children, a child with anger overload sometimes gets so angry that it can take an hour or more for him to calm down. Not only is the angry episode lengthy, but also the level of anger is greater than normal: swearing, hitting, kicking and throwing things is not uncommon for children who experience anger overload. The parents in this situation decided to eliminate video games on weeknights because their child continually had difficulty stopping and getting ready for bed. They avoided the meltdowns by planning ahead and altering the routine in order to prevent anger from escalating. However, sometimes a child's anger will escalate without warning, and there may not be a trigger yet that parents can discern. Planning ahead works if you know there is a pattern, but you will need other techniques for the times you cannot predict!

Help your child with underlying insecurities

Jason's parents noticed he would come home in a bad mood some days from school and be more likely to explode at home those evenings. The parents eventually figured out that some days Jason would get his feelings hurt in school, because his peers either teased him or left him out of an activity that day. For example, if his peers planned to play ball after school and did not invite Jason, he came home with a chip on his shoulder. The parents tried to help soothe Jason's hurt feelings: when they sensed he was upset about something after school, they encouraged him to talk about it, and the parents were empathic. They mentioned that they understood how his feelings could be hurt. They also encouraged him to be more assertive at school. Specifically they suggested when the kids were planning a game he ask one of the boys whom he liked if he could play too. If there was no one he felt comfortable asking, or if the game had already started, he should try to plan something with another boy who was on the sidelines. Regarding after school activities, his parents told him that he could always invite someone to come over and play (without asking his parents in advance). The parents knew how important it was for Jason to have friends, and they did what they could to facilitate that.

If your child has some other issue that underlies some of his episodes of anger overload, you would want to try to address it. One issue that came up for some of Don's episodes of anger was his small stature. Don did not like being small for his age, and a number of tantrums occurred when Don expected to be able to do something like his older brother, but was not able to yet (e.g. skate board without falling, beat his brother in wrestling or video games). It was important to reassure Don that he would have a growth spurt in the next few years and to recommend that for the time being he not engage in as many competitive games with his brother or bigger neighbors (unless he was okay with losing). Parents began to remind Don *before* he played with the neighbors, and at the same time reassured him that someday he was going to be a lot bigger.

Some children have learning problems along with anger overload. One child, a ten year old, would frequently get very upset during homework when she did not know how to do something. She would rip up her paper, throw her book on the floor, scream that she hated her life, and sometimes yell that she hated her parents. Often the outburst would persist with complaining and crying for a half hour or more. In this case, the parents and teacher met and came up with a plan: first of all, they lowered the expectations for the homework. The teacher made some of the homework optional, and the parents and teacher told the child repeatedly that she should just do what she can, and that it was okay to make a lot of mistakes. In addition, the parents hired an educational therapist to work with the child after school several days a week.

By preparing the child ahead of time and by altering the requirements, the parents helped lessen their child's frustration and emotional outbursts.

For many of these children, the parents were able to reduce the frequency of anger episodes by noticing a pattern and taking action before their child would get frustrated. It takes time to notice patterns in your child's behavior, and it takes practice to know when to insert yourself in the sequence before your child gets frustrated. Also, there will be many occasions where you cannot predict your child's behavior, and in the next sections I offer other tools that you can use to help alter your child's tantrums.

Keep reading the next few sections. Then you will come to chart #3, where you will choose which of these strategies to use with your child.

Early anger phase: Emotional distraction and calming strategies

Emotional distraction

When a child is in the midst of anger overload, it is difficult to change his emotional state because the anger is so powerful at that point. However, if you can catch it early while your child is still revving up, you could try to make an amusing or unexpected comment that might change your child's emotional set. Your comment does not have to make logical sense (outlandish statements sometimes work well) because you are not trying to communicate with your child's rational brain. Rather, you are trying to communicate with your child's emotional brain. Examples of "emotional distractions" are singing a lyric or telling a wisecrack about yourself that might make your child smile or laugh. Do not make a joke about your child, as he will likely take offense if he is already in a foul mood. While you sing, crack a joke, or talk about some unusual event (real or fantasy), you could use facial expressions that are weird or unusual for you. Visual images often reach a person's emotional brain better than words. Think of late night comedians, Conan O'Brien or David Letterman, and how when they tell a story their facial expressions change. Part of what we react to when we laugh is their expressions.

Think of what your child is interested in or what he might find amusing. For example, "poop" jokes work with younger children: you could say that you think there might have been an elephant pooping on your front yard yesterday because there was this huge pile of poop. Or, if your child is into computer games, you might say that you wonder if someday there will be a computer that would fit inside your skin so that you could play video games in school without the teacher knowing it. Use your imagination to come up with something that will grab your child's attention. The idea is to get your child wondering about something or laughing. If you can get your child to think about something else, or if you can get him to smile or laugh, his anger will diminish greatly. It is hard to be angry and laugh at the same time!

The other kind of distraction is an activity that your child likes so much that he forgets what he was upset about. For example, you could say you want to bake something for dessert, or maybe you could say that you are going to start a project that your child also enjoys (like building "legos," computer games, wood working, or an art project). You could then start getting ready for the activity, and your child will probably want to come, or you could ask for his help. There is a risk of asking your child a question though if he is still mad; he might say no because of his angry state. So you are usually better off just starting an activity rather than asking for help directly. If your child does not follow, you have left the scene at least, and your child is more likely to calm down if he is by himself. If your child asks to help you, just say fine or "cool", and do not bring back up what he had been angry about. Activities, like baking or playing games, are engrossing and change your child's emotional set, so his anger will diminish or disappear if he gets engaged.

Calming strategies

Another approach that can change your child's emotional set is a calming activity. Is there a soothing activity or calming place in your house? For a younger child, maybe you can set up an area in your child's room or the family room with a mat, a blanket, and some pillows. You can practice in advance making this a fun and soothing place for your child by sometimes playing with him there. Have him lie on the mat and then you could wrap him in a blanket if he likes the feeling of being "hugged." If your child becomes accustomed to this place as a "chill zone" he may be willing to go there if he begins to get frustrated about something. He is more likely to agree when he is frustrated if you practice for several weeks when he is calm and make it a fun place to be. If he does not think to use the chill zone on his own when he is upset, you would cue your child before he gets too angry (if you catch it in time). You could have a verbal cue like "let's chill."

There are other calming activities, such as putting on your child's favorite music or even suggesting he play a video game. This often works well with teenagers. It does not have to be a "peaceful" game, just one that is engrossing for your child and therefore distracting and calming for him. The key is that the activity changes your child's emotional set. Another more traditional calming technique is deep breathing, as slow deep breaths have calming effects on people. Practice for a few weeks taking deep breaths with your child when everyone is calm, before suggesting it when he is upset.

Your child will be more likely to try one of these activities if he is not yet in full anger overload. When children are having a complete meltdown, they will not generally cooperate with anything you suggest.

Overload phase: Ignore or restrain?

When to ignore

Once your child is beyond distraction and is in a full meltdown, usually the best thing for parents to do is *nothing.* As long as your child is not hurting anyone and not breaking things of value or importance to you, you should try to wait out his rage. (e.g. You would intervene if he tries to throw your expensive figurine in the living room, but not if he rips one of his posters off his wall.) Wait for the overload phase to pass. Anything you say during the overload phase is likely to be met with an angry reaction from your child. So do not add to your child's anger. Try to get busy doing something else, and ignore your child as best you can.

It is going to be hard for you to ignore your child if he spouts hateful words while he is in anger overload. You may feel quite hurt, angry, and even horrified by your child's choice of words. Remember that when children (or adults for that matter) are extremely angry, they often say the meanest things that come to their minds at the time. They are not thinking rationally, and what comes out of their mouths is not how they truly feel. Think of their words as "verbal diarrhea." If your child is saying hateful things, try your best not to react and say something back, because anything you say at this point may prolong your child's outburst. Any response would be giving your child your attention, and that would inadvertently reinforce his negative behavior. I know it is going to be difficult not to react. During these episodes, it is not uncommon to feel like grabbing your child or slapping him. Hold on. Try to become temporarily "deaf" to your child's words, and see if you can get some space away from your child until everyone calms down.

Sometimes you are not sure if your child is still reachable or in overload, and if you try a distracting comment and it does not work, do not blame yourself. But if it does not work, just try to back off and leave your child alone. If he has learned to calm himself in his room or in a "chill zone" in the house, maybe he will eventually go there until he is calmer. Or maybe he will stay where he is and continue raging until he runs out of steam. In either case, once your child calms down, *then* listen to what he has to say. Show interest when he is calm. Besides showing him that you care about him, your interest communicates to him that calm behavior is going to get more attention and respect in your house than angry outbursts. Your attention serves as positive reinforcement, and it will help your child learn to calm down more quickly.

When to restrain

Sometimes parents cannot stand by and ignore their child's outbursts. If your child is physically hurting someone in the family, or harming himself, then you will need to intervene and restrain your child. Safety comes first. Also, if your child is trying to destroy something of value, like art objects or figurines in the living room, then you will also need to intervene. Sometimes it is possible to yell "stop" and take the item away from your child. However, if your child continues to try to destroy other items of value to you, then you will need to restrain him. You can hold him in a bear hug, or pin him to the floor. You can do this with younger children, and Don's parents would do this when Don picked up figurines in the living room or when he started to kick his parents. Don was only eight years old and still small. However, Jason was fourteen and bigger than his mother. She could not restrain him when he threw toys at her or kicked his sister. One day when Jason was out of control, the mother called the police, who came and talked to him. After that, Mom told Jason she would not hesitate to call the police if he became violent again. As a result, there were many fewer incidents of physical violence, though verbal outbursts did not diminish yet.

When to use praise and consequences

When to praise

When your child tries to use a calming technique, for example, he goes to his room or the "chill zone" in your house, then after the outburst is over, it is important to verbally praise your child for his efforts. You do this even if the child was out of control and said some awful things before he went to the chill zone. This does not mean you are endorsing his verbal attacks, just his efforts to contain his anger.

Praise is important because it communicates you appreciate his effort. When a child begins to use a new behavior (that is adaptive) you want to communicate your approval, even if the behavior is not ideal yet. Behavioral psychologists call this "shaping." You are praising approximations to the goal, because it is hard for your child to have complete self-control all at once. As the weeks go by, you may be less effusive in your praise unless your child continues to improve his efforts, e.g. go to the chill zone more quickly. When there is again improvement, you notice it and make special mention of it.

It is also a good idea to praise your child if, rather than swearing, he uses more appropriate language, such as telling you what he does not like. Sometimes a child will do this on his own after he calms down.

I used to encourage parents to teach more appropriate language, because I thought that if children learned more appropriate words, they would use them when they were angry. However, I found that children with anger overload did not have fewer tantrums after parents coached their children to use "better" words. Children were not able to use new, more appropriate words because their level of arousal would get so high. Most children know what the more acceptable words are, but do not use them during anger overload. It is more important therefore for parents to focus on strategies that lower a child's arousal level. The more appropriate words will come out of your child's mouth when he is not so angry!

Do incentives and consequences help?

During a meltdown, it is generally not helpful to impose consequences. Your child is not acting rationally at the moment, and consequences will not have a positive effect. Remember that anything you say during a meltdown may increase your child's anger and possibly lengthen his meltdown.

Sometimes parents feel it is important to have a negative consequence, particularly if important house rules were violated, such as swearing at you or breaking something of value. Parents want also to send a signal to their other children that they will pay a price if they copy their sibling and act in an extremely negative way. If you are going to use a consequence, you could explain what some possibilities are ahead of time when everyone is calm. But, do not mention it during your child's meltdown, or you will likely aggravate the situation. Wait until things have calmed down. If you find that you child revs back up when you impose a consequence, then you might want to wait longer next time, maybe until the next morning. Some children need longer to totally calm down.

One possible penalty is to pay for what was broken. Another is to lose privileges for a day or two, such as driving the car (for older teens) or playing outside or playing video games (for younger children). If you are going to use a consequence, pick one that you think will be meaningful for your child. Also, it is recommended that the consequence not go on for a week or longer. If it is a long consequence, you cannot use it again if there is another severe outburst later in the week. Besides, if your choice of consequence is truly meaningful to your child, it will usually have an effect if imposed for just a day. You will know in the weeks to come if it was effective because there will be a decrease in the frequency or intensity of angry behaviors in the type of situation where you have used a consequence. Your child may say he does not care about the consequence, but he may just be trying to act tough and invulnerable; what really matters is what happens in the following few weeks. Does he attempt to control his behavior? For example, Jason's parents noticed a significant decrease in violent behavior after the police were called. That served as an effective negative consequence for Jason.

Possible incentives include earning movie or game time on Friday nights (at the end of the week) or a favorite card game each evening if your child makes an effort to control his anger. You would need to define in advance what would constitute "self-control:" you could decide that the goal would be no tantrums at all, or the goal could be no more than one or two tantrums a week. Set the goal as some improvement, but not total self-control if your child is currently having many tantrums a day. For younger and more explosive children, have daily incentives, rather than waiting until the end of the week.

Some children have more control than others, and will modify their behavior to avoid a significant consequence or to earn a reward. Ultimately you must decide what you think will help your child. I would recommend you concentrate first on the other techniques I am suggesting, because these will lessen the severity of your child's outbursts. If your child is less emotional, then he will be more capable of thinking rationally about incentives and consequences, and it is then more likely that he will try to control his anger.

I want to point out that even if you decide not to take anything away from your child it does not mean you are failing to send a signal to your child about his behavior. By ignoring him during his tantrum, you have used the withdrawal of your attention as a negative consequence. Children care a lot about your time and attention, even if they will not admit it. So if you do not say anything during an outburst, you are sending a signal to your child. Then when your child has calmed down, you resume paying attention to him. In essence, you are using yourself as the primary means of reinforcement for your child.

Now I want you to plan your strategy for the next times your child gets angry. Try to come up with a list of tools for each kind of situation you face with your child. Use chart #3 to help organize your thinking.

Chart 3: For each situation, what is my strategy?

I. One situation where there has been anger overload in the last two weeks:

____

____

Prevention:

How could I prepare my child in advance and lower expectations?

____

Could I alter the routine and avoid the trigger?

____

Is my child insecure about something and does that underlie these outbursts?

____

Early anger phase:

Possible emotional distractions:

____

Possible calming strategies: ______________________________

Overload phase:

Do I ignore or restrain? ______________

Will I use a consequence (afterwards) and what will it be?

____

Will I use an incentive if there are fewer outbursts? ____________________

II. Another situation where there has been anger overload in the last two weeks:

____

____

Prevention:

How could I prepare my child in advance? ______________________

Could I alter the routine and avoid the trigger?

____

Is my child insecure about something and does that underlie these outbursts?

____

Early anger phase:

Possible emotional distractions:

____

Possible calming strategies: ______________________

Overload phase:

Do I ignore or restrain? __________

Will I use a consequence (afterwards) and what will it be?

____

Will I use an incentive if there are fewer outbursts? ______________________

You can plan for more than two situations if you want. There are extra blank recording sheets for chart #3 in the appendix. What most parents do is work on two situations at a time. After a couple of weeks if you are making progress, you can work on another situation as well. If some strategies are not helping, alter or drop them from your "arsenal." Continue using these behavior plans for the coming month. Also read the next step on being a role model.

Be a role model

You are the most important person in your child's life. What you do has a great impact on your child. If you model self-control, this will mean a lot to your child. Over time, he will try to imitate you. This does not mean it will happen the next day. But you will see a difference over a period of several months.

Here is what you could do: When you get annoyed or angry, see if you can verbalize what was the trigger and what you are going to do to calm down. It may be hard to do this when you are really riled up. So wait until you are calmer. You want to pick a time when you can speak dispassionately about what happened. And you want to pick a time that your child is around and listening—maybe at a meal, but not while he is in the middle of a television show or video game.

You will be illustrating for your child that he is not the only one in the family who gets angry and who is working on calming strategies. If you chose to do a calming activity, like go on the computer, or start cooking dinner, and this helped you calm down, then you could say this later when you speak with your child. Keep it short and simple. Your child will tune you out if you go on at length.

If you fly off the handle and do not have a reliable calming strategy, then you need to work on this! Since you are a role model, if you have explosions and have not figured out what to do about them, you cannot expect your child to learn how to calm down. The way you handle your anger serves as an example for your child to follow, whether good or bad!

If you can illustrate a couple of times a week what you do to chill when you get angry, this will help your child develop his own calming skills. Your child may not choose the exact same techniques, but may pick a strategy more in keeping with his age. The key is that your child sees you trying. Even if you do not have a lot of trouble with anger, you can still model calming strategies when you do get angry. Keep a chart like the one below of your triggers and your strategies. Then indicate with a check mark how often you used the strategy and also how often you later explained it to your child. There should be as many check marks for verbalizing your strategy as there are for using the strategy. By doing both, you are increasing the impact of your behavior on your child.

One caution about this strategy: Do not pick serious marital conflicts to use for examples. Many children get anxious if their parents have major conflicts, so you do not want to focus on these problems with your children.

Chart 4: Modeling a calming strategy

What you said or did:

____

What was the trigger (the situation and why you think it affected you)?

____

What you did to calm down: ____

How often this week you used the strategy: _________________________

How often this week you verbalized to your child the trigger and/or the strategy:

____

Use all of what you have learned to this point for one to two months before starting part 2 of the manual. In part 2, "Teaching your child new skills," your child will learn new skills to cope with anger. Before you get to this point you want your child's anger to be eased somewhat. Ask yourself if there are some times when your child gets angry but is not totally out of control. If your answer is yes, then you are ready for part 2.

Part 2: Teaching your child new skills

First step: Review patterns and explain rationale

Now you are going to embark on a program to teach your child to observe more closely his behavior and to open his mind to new ways of looking at situations that have provoked his rage. The techniques you are going to teach your child come out of what is called the cognitive-behavioral field of psychology. The underlying premise is that if people change the way they look at things, they will better be able to deal with difficult situations. We are going to apply cognitive behavioral principles to anger overload in children. I am going to show you how to do this work with your child. Since your child mostly gets angry at home, you witness (more than any other adult) what triggers his rage. Now you will learn how to help him change the way he views these triggers, and in the process your child will develop more control of his anger.

There are two important ideas to keep in mind as you implement these cognitive strategies. As your child's "emotional teacher," you must remain *patient* and *empathic*. It takes time to implement the program that follows. Do not rush through the steps. You will see that I ask you to fill out many of the worksheets repeatedly with your child over a number of weeks. I will explain in each section how long to use one worksheet before going on to the next. The reason you must work slowly with your child is that you want him to understand and begin to internalize each strategy (for it to become a habit) before moving on to the next. It may sometimes seem boring and repetitious to you, but it is crucial to take the time filling out the worksheets with your child, so that he truly "gets the message."

Also, you want your child to feel that you are embarking on a project together, in which his views are important. As you fill out the worksheets together be sure to listen to your child's opinions and consider seriously his ideas. Even if his thoughts are not exactly accurate in your view, try to incorporate your child's ideas. Your child will be more engaged in the process and more likely to accept your help if you listen as well as teach. The key word here is empathy. Be understanding that this is not easy for your child. Anger overload is tough to control. Your child is struggling with it as much as you are struggling to help him. Okay, let's move on now to the first step.

First review chart #1, which you filled out at the beginning of this manual. It outlines situations when your child has experienced anger overload. Pick a time when your child is calm and not preoccupied. Dinnertime, or the period before bedtime, is often a quiet time when you can speak with your child about important matters. Explain that the two of you (or three of you, including your spouse) are going to be a team that is going to work on anger in the family. Give him an example from chart #1. (Use the chart to organize your thoughts but do not read from the chart or show it to your child at this time.) Also, try to give an example of when you got angry. Explain you are going to work on your anger and you will also help your child work on his. By explaining the program in this way, you make it a joint project and do not single out your child, which might have made him feel criticized. He is more likely to be a partner with you if he does not feel put down from the start.

You could also say that the program you will be working on together comes from a book written by a doctor who helps families. This gives the program more significance: a doctor developed it, and it has helped many families already. You could add that the program teaches important skills that "we can use in our family as well as with our friends and in our jobs. If we can control our anger better, other people will respect us and listen better to us. They will be less likely to shy away from us." Here you are adding to the rationale for working on anger: not only will it help the family but also help each of us outside the family. Most children want to be respected and want to be popular. So mentioning how your work together will help him be respected by his peers will be appealing.

You could also acknowledge that it is hard to control anger. It is a strong emotion, and it is going to take a lot of work to keep it from exploding. "When we get frustrated, we tend to get angry right away. Some people are quicker to anger than others, so that makes it more of a challenge to control it. But that also means it will be a real accomplishment when we learn how to control it. It gets easier with practice. It's like learning anything, playing ball, riding a bike, learning to write: the more we practice the better we get. So in the coming weeks, we are going to practice together."

Now it is time to discuss (in a little more detail) one example when your child got angry and also one example when you have gotten angry. Mention first a time when you got angry, what triggered it, and what you said. Explain that you wish you could have done something a little different and say what that is. Now mention a time your child got angry and what he said or did. Pick something that your child will remember. Then say these are the kinds of things we are going to change. You are setting the scene, but not demanding anything of your child yet. If he has ideas, and wants to comment, terrific! Acknowledge his input and tie it in to the goal (which is working on anger and improving self-control) that you have set for the family.

For some children it also helps to mention childhood heroes and how they cope with anger. For example, my children admired Michael Jordan. We live in Chicago and heard about his basketball performance for years. One story about Michael was that if he had a bad night, and some player bested him, he did not push the player or knock him down, and possibly get thrown out of the game. Instead he channeled his anger, and the next time they played, he played even harder and usually had a great game. He showed what he could do by focusing and trying harder rather than exploding. You could mention this story, or if your child has a hero, try to use the hero's behavior to illustrate the idea of self-control and its value.

Second step: Develop self-observation skills

Choose a labeling system

It will be easier to regulate anger, if you and your child recognize early stages when anger is not as elevated. Many children pass through the stages quickly without recognizing their feelings. It is important therefore to teach children to see that there are different levels of anger, not just the explosive stage of anger overload. If they learn to recognize the early stages there will be more they can do to control it.

There are different labels we can use for the levels of anger. You want to pick a labeling system that you think will make the most sense to your child. Some parents like to use the colors of a fire: from low level "blue," to middle level "orange," to "red" hot. Other children relate better to the speed of a race car: low level being 30 miles per hour, medium fast being highway speed of 60 miles per hour, and super fast being 90 miles per hour. Other metaphors that may be appealing to your child: storms (little rain, thunder storm, and tornado), or the height of mountains (hill, mountain, sky high). Still other children pay attention better to nonverbal labels: holding your index finger up in the air for the first level, then putting up all the fingers of one hand, for the next level, and two hands up for the highest level of anger. When everyone in the family is calm one day, mention a few possibilities and ask your child if he has a preference. Then pick a labeling system together. Notice that each labeling system essentially has three levels: low, medium and high. This allows for a range for describing anger, but it is not too cumbersome to use.

Now give an example of anger at each of the three levels. For the highest level, give an example of someone screaming and using words that express total disregard and disrespect for the other person ("you're full of sh**" or "I hate you.") and while saying this, make a menacing facial expression. Another possibility for the highest level of anger is to pretend to throw or kick something. Pick whatever is consistent with what your child might do when he is extremely angry. For the middle level, give an example of someone raising his voice and maybe even being sarcastic but speaking with less vehemence and rage (no screaming "I hate you" but it's okay to say "I hate that") and without becoming physically violent. For the lowest level, use words that express feelings of anger or displeasure ("I'm mad," "That's so unfair," or "Come on, anything but that.") but in a moderate tone (no screaming) and without verbally putting down the other person. When you present examples of each level of anger, be sure to use phrases or behaviors that make sense for your child. If he does not swear at you, for instance, do not use that as an example of extreme anger. Pick what he typically does instead. Also, remember that expressions of anger will have some emotional words even at the middle and lower levels, which is why I included "I hate that" (but not "I hate you!") as an example for the middle level. You do not have to use that example though for your child if that is not something he would say.

Once you have established a labeling system, you begin recording at night together (see chart #5 below) what the person said or did in anger and also the level of anger. Write down the sequence of angry statements or actions, and for each statement indicate what was the level of anger. You would use the labels you have already chosen for the three levels of anger. Sometimes the level of anger will stay the same throughout the entire incident, but often it will build toward a climax. You want your child to see that anger can come in different degrees.

If both you and your child got angry, then fill in situation #1 in chart 5 for you, and use #2 for your child. Or if only one person got angry, but it happened multiple times in a day, then use situations #1 and #2 for different bouts of anger during the day. The reason why we keep track at night (or later in the day) is that it helps children to develop self-observation skills if they review situations when they are calmer. You also have a written record that we are going to use in the steps that follow.

Tie in any bodily sensations

In addition, you ask your child (or whoever else got angry) if he noticed any signs in his body when he got angry. Were there any physical indicators of anger, and, if so, does he know at what point they began? For example, some people get tightness in their chest or stomach, some people breathe more rapidly, some people feel a pain in their stomach or head, and others notice increased sweating. Ask your child if he noticed any of these, or if he noticed anything else in his body or head when he got angry. Does he know when he began having those physical sensations? What was the level of his anger at the time? Sometimes it is hard to remember when the physical feelings started, especially if the angry sequence went on for many minutes. For example, a person could start out arguing, then start yelling, and finally throw things; it might be hard to identify when the bodily sensations started in that sequence. That's okay. It's also quite possible that no one noticed any physical sensations; in that case just leave that part of chart #5 blank.

Type of trigger

One more thing you will record at this point in chart #5, and that is the type of trigger. I want you and your child to come up with a category or theme for each situation when someone got angry. There can be a different theme for each situation, or it may be similar. You can come up with any categories that make sense to you and your child, or you can adapt ones that I have used with other families: "not getting to do what I want," "being treated unfairly," or "my feelings were hurt."

When you write down the trigger in chart #5, describe the type of activity that your child reacted to, as well as the theme for how he felt about it. Here are some examples: "not getting to play video games when he wanted," "being treated unfairly when there was a fight with his brother," or "getting frustrated with himself when he didn't skate as well as he wanted." This process of identifying triggers helps everyone focus on the precipitants of a person's rage. The triggers will also be very important later on when you will try to change the way your child looks at things.

Chart 5: Level of anger and bodily sensations

Situation 1: Who got angry? ________________________________

What was the sequence of his (or her) angry statements or behaviors?

a)____ Level______

b)____ Level______

c)____ Level_______

Any bodily sensations, and if so, when did they start? ____________________________________

Looking back, what was the trigger? ____

Situation 2: Who got angry? ____________________

What was the sequence of his (or her) angry statements or behaviors?

a)____ Level ______

b)____ Level ______

c)____ Level ______

Any bodily sensations, and if so, when did they start? ___________________________________

Looking back, what was the trigger? ____

Now we have discussed all the parts of chart #5. Try to do a page at night whenever there has been an outburst. By writing down what happened that day, everyone gets a clearer picture of what was happening when someone got angry. Awareness is a big part of change, so try to follow through with the charting, and you will see greater progress in the future. Work on the chart together. Sometimes ask your child what he thinks, especially on items that do not require interpretation, e.g. ask him who he was angry at, what was said, and whether he felt anything in his body. If your child has any bodily sensations associated with the early or middle levels of anger, explain that he can use these bodily sensations as early warning signs that he is getting close to anger overload. When you come to the question about the triggering event, you will probably need to suggest a theme to your child. It will be hard for a child to figure this out himself. Say out loud what you think the theme is, so your child can hear and think about it.

If your child does not want to help some nights, still try to write in your observations while your child is present. While you are writing, say some of your observations out loud. Also, it is helpful to do this quickly, in about five minutes, and go on to something your child enjoys, like a story or a card game. If you always follow the charting with a fun activity, and you keep the charting brief, then you will get greater compliance. If your child has an outburst about the charting then do it later yourself, and skip the fun activity that night.

Fill out chart #5 with your child over the next two weeks. There are extra copies of chart #5 in the appendix. Do not go on to the next step until you and your child have grown accustomed to the labeling system and have identified some of the triggers together. You should also be continuing to use the parenting strategies that you learned in part 1. After a couple of weeks, go on to the next step: "Use labels together with calming strategies."

Third step: Use labels together with calming strategies

Use labels at the time of upset

After a couple of weeks charting the levels of anger with your child in the evening (when everyone is calm), you are ready to begin to use the labels at the time a person is angry. This will help everyone to become increasingly aware of the levels of anger being expressed in the family. If you or your child becomes angry, see if you can calmly label the level of anger with words, or hand signals, without judging or criticizing the person. The person who is getting angry is likely to be sensitive to this, but hopefully has gotten used to the idea through the nightly charting (which you have already done for a couple of weeks). You should not argue if your child disagrees with a label. Also, do not expect an acknowledgement from your child that you are right. Over a period of several months, your child will learn to recognize the levels of his anger.

By the way, you should also continue the nightly charting (using chart #5) because it will keep reinforcing the labeling process and also help you fine-tune what the triggers are. The nighttime charting is where you can talk calmly with your child about what happened if he got angry that day. Remember you do not want to say too much at the time of anger overload. You just use a brief label at the time of the outburst to try to increase everyone's awareness. If your child is extremely angry and escalates further when you mention a label, then hold off labeling at the time of extreme anger, but continue labeling the lower levels of anger.

At the time your child is angry, it is wise to verbalize just one or two labels per incident, even if the level of anger changes a lot during the incident. Some children get increasingly angry if many of their statements are labeled, whereas other children tolerate their parents changing the label as the level of anger changes. See how your child responds to the verbal labels, and decide how many labels per incident your child can tolerate. You do not want to pay too much attention to your child during his angry outbursts, and you do not want to add to his anger, so for most children it is better not to label everything they say or do.

Use the labels at the time of upset for a week before going on to the next step. You want to make sure your child is comfortable with hearing the labels when he is angry, before you introduce a calming strategy.

Distract or suggest calming strategy

Here is where you can integrate the labeling system with the calming strategies we suggested earlier. (Take a look back at chart #3, and review your calming strategies.) After you use a label, sometimes suggest to your child that he try to use his chill zone (or other calming technique you have worked on with him in part one of the manual). If it is hard for him to calm himself at this point, then another option is for you to try distracting him. (See what distracting strategy you have written down in chart #3 and try it after labeling the level of anger.) For example, talk about something that might change your child's emotion from anger to amusement or wonder. Talk, or ask, about something amusing or mystifying to your child (e.g., If he likes fast cars, ask him whether the latest model Lamborghini has good fuel mileage? Or if he likes space exploration, ask him how long he thinks before scientists can detect life in another solar system.) Whatever you ask or say, you should use a tone of voice that indicates you are really wondering about the topic yourself. If your child does not seem to respond well to these kinds of comments, then try to involve your child in a fun activity (e.g. Most children like to bake desserts, or play a fun game together.) All these suggestions are more likely to work if you caught the level of anger before it reached the highest level. Once your child is in complete overload, it is usually best to say little or nothing at all. This is when you ignore your child, unless he is harming himself or someone else.

If your child had any bodily sensations at an early or middle stage of anger (look back at chart #5), then tell your child to be on the look out for these early warning signs. Mention that his physical feelings give him a clue that he is getting angry. Explain that once he recognizes this, he could try to chill (in whatever way you and he think would work best for him).

Continue to use labels as well as calming and distracting strategies over the next month. You want your child to build awareness and realize there are alternatives to his outbursts. If you make this a focus for the month, your child will become increasingly aware of the level of his anger, and he may sometimes be willing to use a calming strategy.

Wait at least a month before going on to the fourth step. The more your child learns to observe his anger, the more likely he will be cooperative with the next stage: "Teach your child about other points of view."

Fourth step: Teach your child about other points of view

Explain how new information can change your opinion

Now you are going to teach your child how our anger depends on how we evaluate situations, which in turn depends on the kind of information we have. When we find out new facts, our opinions can change. The "new facts" we want your child to consider are other people's views of the situations that arouse anger. Your goal is to help your child think about how other people view things, and to use this information before he becomes enraged.

In chart #6, you will look at two kinds of situations with your child. These types of situations are those that frequently cause anger overload. The first situation in chart #6 is about disappointment when a person does not get to do what he expected or wanted. We will use the example of Don expecting to have a catch with his dad in the backyard after the parents get home from work. But when the parents get home, they say that they can't have a catch tonight.

Describe the situation to your child and ask him how he thinks Don feels. Your child will probably say that Don is angry. Then I want you to explain that it turns out the dad hurt his back at work that day and needed to lie down after dinner to rest his back. He tells this to Don later at the dinner table. Now ask your child how he thinks Don feels. Your child may think Don would be a bit more understanding of the father, but may wonder why the father did not say this right away. Or your child may think the father is exaggerating to get out of having a catch. Your child may still empathize primarily with Don, but hopefully he sees that there is another side to the story. You could say that it helps to see things from the father's point of view as well as the child's in order to better understand why things did not work out. You or your child could now write down his answers in chart #6 before going on to the second story.

In the second example, we use something that happened to the teenager Jason whom we have spoken about earlier. You ask how Jason feels about his parents telling him to give his sister a turn on the computer while he is "Facebooking" his friends. Your child will probably say that Jason is angry or that it is not fair that his parents want him to stop what he is doing. Next explain what happened to the sister that day, that she had a doctor's appointment and got home late and did not have a chance to use the computer yet. Usually she has a turn earlier in the afternoon before Jason gets home from school. Ask your child how Jason feels after the mother explained what happened to the sister. See if your child's opinion changes. Your child may still feel it is unfair for Jason to have to stop what he is doing on the computer, but may realize why the parent has told Jason to give his sister a turn. You want to emphasize how the new information changes things somewhat, even if your child still empathizes with Jason. Finish filling out chart #6 with your child.

Chart 6: How new information affects Don and Jason's anger

1. Don is disappointed.

The situation: Don is expecting to have a catch with his dad after his parents get home from work.

How do you think Don feels after his father says he can't have a catch tonight?

____

New information: Don finds out his parent's back is sore.

How does Don feel now? ____

2. Jason thinks his parents are not fair.

The situation: Jason is in the midst of "Facebooking" his friends when his parent says it is time to give his sister a turn. Jason thinks his sister has already had a turn today.

How does Jason feel? ____

New information: Jason finds out his sister had a doctor's appointment after school and did not get on the computer yet.

How does Jason feel now? ____

Now think of two situations when your child was angry during the past week. You will use these situations to fill out chart #7. If it is hard for either you or your child to remember the details of an outburst in the last week, then wait until the next outburst occurs and fill out the first situation for chart #7 later that day, after everyone has calmed down. Pick a situation in which your child reacted before hearing, or thinking over, all the "facts." This will be true most of the time someone experiences anger overload. In most situations when there is anger overload, the person has a narrow focus: he thinks that something has been unfairly done to him, and he does not yet fully appreciate that other people may have another way of looking at the situation. Sit down with your child when everyone is calm, and fill out the first section of chart #7. (You can finish filling out this chart another day when you have another outburst to record.) For many children, it would be helpful if you also fill out the chart for a situation in which you got angry. This enables your child to see that everyone, not just he, has trouble with anger at times. The main point of this exercise is to help him see that when each of you considers all the facts, your feelings change, at least somewhat.

Chart 7: How new information affects anger in your family

Situation 1: ____

Who was the target of your child's anger? ______________________________

What did your child say or do? ______________________________

What did your child find out (or realize) later? ______________________________

How did your child feel then? ______________________________

Situation 2: ____

Who was the target of your child's anger? ______________________________

What did your child say or do? ______________________________

What did your child find out (or realize) later? ______________________________

How did your child feel then? ______________________________

Situation 3: When you (one of the parents) got angry: ______________________________

Who was the target of your anger? ______________________________

What did you say or do? ______________________________

What did you find out (realize) later? ______________________________

How did you feel then? ____

Wait a couple of weeks and work on chart #7 with your child. There are extra copies in the appendix. In the next section you will learn about using catch phrases. You will see that these two strategies—looking at different points of view and using catch phrases—go hand in hand.

Fifth step: Use catch phrases to help your child think before reacting

It is going to be hard for your child to remember the importance of thinking about different viewpoints when he feels disappointed or frustrated. When your child gets emotional, his focus is going to be on his own feelings. So what you need to do now is to develop a catch phrase (or words) that will help your child to stop and think. Some examples of meaningful catch phrases are "Wait. Let me think first," or "There is more than one way to look at this," or "What's another way to look at this?" or "They must have a reason" or "Other people have feelings too." You and your child should decide whether you like one of these or whether you prefer one of your own. It should be a phrase your child is comfortable with. Give him several examples and ask him to choose one, or ask him what's another phrase that would help him to think first.

Whichever phrase is chosen, you will also want to use it yourself whenever you are getting angry. You want to continue to serve as a role model for your child, as this will increase the likelihood that your child will remember to use the catch phrase. Explain that anyone can use the phrase to remind himself to think about a frustrating situation, or can remind someone else in the family to try to think first if one of you is starting to get angry. Explain also that it works better to use the phrase early when you or someone else begins to feel angry, because it is hard to stop and think when you feel *very* angry.

Using a catch phrase is important because it reminds your child to think about other information. Even if your child does not really consider other information yet when he or you say the catch phrase, mentioning the catch phrase still serves to encourage your child to pause. Anything that helps your child to delay the build up of his anger can help head off anger overload. If the emotional fuse does not burn too quickly, your child's rational brain has time to gain control. Do not expect the catch phrase to prevent anger overload for a while. Emotions are powerful and quick, so that it takes time and practice to be able to exert self-control.

Once you have agreed on a catch phrase, in order to help everyone remember it, you and/or your child could make one or two colorful posters with the catch phrase, and hang them in places in the house where your child sometimes gets angry. If you have other children, explain what the posters are about, and say that you hope they can help anyone in the house remember to think about other viewpoints when they get angry.

One final thing to do in order to help everyone remember the catch phrase is to role-play one of the situations in chart #7, and insert the catch phrase before the person gets too angry. You might first play the role of the person who gets angry and pause when you use the catch phrase and act like you are thinking. Then ask your child to take that part. Explain that in real life situations, you do not have to say the catch phrase out loud, but might say it in your head, especially if you are somewhere other than home where people may not understand why you are mentioning the catch phrase. Compliment your child after each of you takes a turn acting out the use of a catch phrase. Was either of you less angry in the role-play after you stopped to think? You could point out that the catch phrase will eventually help each of you to handle your anger in a less explosive way. Explain that you may not think about other ways of looking at things when you first try using catch phrases, but that someday something will occur to you and help you to stay calm.

Now everyone in the family should be on the lookout for opportunities to use the catch phrase when you see yourself starting to get angry or when you see someone else in the family getting angry. It is important that anyone who mentions the catch phrase does so calmly and non-critically. The person getting angry will be sensitive if he feels criticized. When you use the catch phrase, you *do not* also mention out loud what the person's level of anger is. You want to keep your words brief when someone is angry, and you want your child at this point in the training to focus on the catch phrase rather than the level of anger.

Over the next few weeks keep track of when you or your child mentioned the catch phrase. Write down who suggested the catch phrase and who was getting angry at the time. I have organized this information for you in chart #8. You might fill this out at night after dinner when everyone is calm. You want to use this chart the same day as the catch phrase was used, so that it is more likely everyone will remember the situation. However, you want to be sure everyone has calmed down before reviewing what happened. (Note that chart #8 is an adaptation of chart #5, and should be used in place of chart #5 once you get to this point in the manual.)

After a few weeks using chart #8, you could take a look to see if the catch phrase is beginning to have an effect. What did the person say or do after the catch phrase was used? Does the person sometimes have more self-control?

If after a few weeks you are not seeing any changes in your child's level of anger when using catch phrases, try to mention the catch phrase earlier in the sequence. I have found that catch phrases are less likely to help if they come too late in the anger sequence, i.e. if your child is already in full anger overload. Also, try to use an "unusual" facial expression when mentioning the phrase so that you are more likely to catch your child's attention. Your expression could be whimsical or contemplative, but not harsh or critical looking. Be sure to compliment your child if he seems to think a little more. Praise him if he is trying, even if he still has trouble modulating his anger. If you praise small steps, your child will be more likely to take larger steps toward self-control in the weeks to come!

One last thing to take a look at: the trigger. Is it easier for your child to use the catch phrase for some triggers rather than others? Sometimes a trigger is so emotionally charged for a particular child that catch phrases are ineffective. If this is the case for any of your child's triggers, then for that type of situation, give your child time alone to calm down instead. Fall back on the strategies in part one of the manual when your child is too angry to think clearly. You should still talk about what happened at night when everyone is calm, and point out what were the different points of view. Eventually you may be able to use catch phrases for these emotional triggers once your child's level of anger is lower and once you have gone over other points of view enough times that he is primed to think that way. Be patient because for some triggers this may take a month or more.

Chart 8: Using catch phrases

Situation 1: Who got angry with whom? ______________________________

What did the person who got angry say or do? ____________________________

Who mentioned a catch phrase and what was it? ___________________________________

What did the person who got angry say or do next? ________________________

Looking back now, what was the trigger? ____

Looking back now, what was another way of looking at the situation?

____

Situation 2: Who got angry with whom? ___________________

What did the person who got angry say or do? _____________________________

Who mentioned a catch phrase and what was it? __________________________________

What did the person who got angry say or do next? __________________________

Looking back now, what was the trigger? ____

Looking back now, what was another way of looking at the situation?

____

Situation 3: Who got angry with whom? ___________________

What did the person who got angry say or do? _____________________________

Who mentioned a catch phrase and what was it? __________________________________

What did the person who got angry say or do next? ___________________________

Looking back now, what was the trigger? ____

Looking back now, what was another way of looking at the situation?

____

Use chart #8 for the next month. Extra copies are in the appendix. By a month from now, your child will more often recognize that there are alternative points of view. He may not think about other viewpoints until after the anger episode is over, though. But if you keep using the chart for several months, your child will eventually think about other people's views at the time of anger.

Sixth Step: Teach compromise technique

Introduce technique: You feel...I feel...

It is time to teach your child one more technique to prevent blow-ups. In the previous sections, you and your child worked a lot on the idea that people have different points of view. You helped him to see what other people think and to consider this new information (hopefully) before reacting too strongly. Your goal then was to have him change his evaluation of a situation and thereby change his level of emotional arousal. Now you want to show him how it is sometimes possible to find a compromise that takes into account both his point of view and yours. His level of anger will lessen if there is a compromise that both of you can accept.

It is not easy to work on compromise when people are highly aroused. When anger is high, people emote, rather than think. Compromise requires rational thought, so it is only possible if the earlier steps in the manual have helped modulate your child's level of anger, or if you can catch his anger at an early stage. If someone is already in anger overload, then wait and use this technique after everyone has calmed down. The goal in that case is to compromise after the incident in order to prevent future blow-ups.

Explain to your child that you are all going to work on finding compromises where everyone's views are considered. Tell your child that one way to do this is for one of you to state each person's point of view and then suggest a compromise that takes into account both points of view. It can make each person happy, because each person feels he got some of what he wanted. (Furthermore, the process forces everybody to slow down and think about other points of view. When people slow down to think, there is less of a chance for anger overload.)

After you have explained the goal to your child, illustrate the technique using some of the issues Don and Jason faced with their parents. Don was angry that his parent would not go outside to have a catch with him, and Jason was angry that he had to get off the computer in the middle of "Facebooking" and give his sister a turn. Start with Don: state the problem Don had, and ask your child what Don felt. Then ask he if remembered what Don's parent felt. If your child does not remember, then you say that Don's parent came home from work with a backache.

Next pose the question: How can they compromise so they each get something they want? Most children will not come up with a possible compromise right away, so you should suggest a few: have a catch in a couple of days when the parent's back feels better, or play a game inside where the parent can stay seated and not stress his back, or play a game with someone else in the family. Ask your child which alternative he thinks would work better. Support your child's choice unless he comes up with something that does not take into account both points of view.

Have the same kind of discussion with your child about Jason not wanting to get off the computer to give his sister a turn. Ask for possible compromises. If your child mentions one possibility that takes into account both points of view, compliment him. If not, suggest a few possibilities such as: ask for five minutes to finish "Facebooking," ask to go back on the computer later, or ask if next time someone could tell him at breakfast if his sister would be going to the doctor and would not be using the computer right after school. Discuss with your child which compromise sounds best. The purpose of these examples is to give your child the idea of what a compromise could be.

How to reach a compromise in your family

When you are ready to illustrate how this technique could work in your family, think about a situation that you are both familiar with, something that happened fairly recently. Also consider whether the situation lends itself to compromise. Do not pick situations to start where you feel compromise is impossible. For example, if you do not want your child going to bed later then 10 p.m. on school nights, and this is what your child was angry about, do not pick this situation for now.

State a recent situation, and then both of you think of possible compromises. Use chart #9. You can fill out the chart together, or if your child prefers, he can write down his answers on one copy of the chart while you fill out another copy for the same situation. Then look at them together. Do you agree on what the two points of view are? If not, one of you restates the points of view until you both agree on what they are. Next discuss which compromises take into account both points of view. If you can think of a second situation where compromise is possible, then repeat this procedure for the second situation.

Chart 9: Possible compromises

Situation 1: ____

What is your point of view? ______________________________________

What is the other person's point of view? ____________________________

What are possible compromises? ___________________________________

____

Situation 2: ____

What is your point of view? ______________________________________

What is the other person's point of view? ____________________________

What are possible compromises? ___________________________________

____

Now pick one of these situations and role-play. Before you act out the situation, you should write out the script together. You can use what you have written in chart #9 to help with the script. Decide who is going to take which role. Also, decide which of the possible compromises you are going to use for your role-play, and which person is going to propose it. When you have all the details worked out, you are ready to act out the scene. Later in the week, try role-playing the second situation from your chart. If you have not come up with a second situation yet, see if you can do so in the next week or two, and then role-play it.

Use the technique before or after anger overload (but not during overload)

Now you are ready to put the technique to use in a new situation. Pick a time when someone is angry (but not at the highest level of arousal); or if someone is already in overload, wait until everyone is calm before trying the technique. It will not work when people are so angry that it is hard to be rational.

You could start by saying "I notice we are disagreeing on this. Here is what I think each us is saying.... Would you agree that those are our points of view?" If not, ask your child to state both points of view. Once you agree on both points of view, ask (or state) what is a compromise that takes into account both views. A simple question that gets your child to think about a compromise is to ask: "So what do we do?"

If you can compromise, the level of anger should decrease considerably. Compliment your child on being thoughtful and fair. For your part, stay calm and respectful during this process. If you cannot reach a compromise, suggest that each of you think about it and talk again later (or tomorrow). Usually even if a compromise is not reached, the act of having this discussion keeps everyone thinking rationally and limits the likelihood that someone will feel slighted or ignored, either of which could have stimulated anger overload.

Continue to use the compromise technique with your child for the next few months. If your child begins to utilize this technique over time, or any of the other techniques, compliment your child (and yourself). You want this to become a regular part of your child's repertoire. Look back over all the steps in part 2 of the manual: labeling the level of anger, tying in calming techniques, thinking of other points of view, using catch phrases, and learning how to compromise. Which steps have helped your child the most? Continue to use those strategies from now on.

Summary

Anger is a strong emotion, and without continued practice, it is possible your child will regress. So keep using the strategies that are working. Furthermore, keep in mind that even if your child is doing better, once in a while he may still have an explosion. Do not despair. Your goal is to reduce the frequency and intensity of anger overload. Over time the frequency and intensity will lessen some more.

For some children there will be no change for the first few months. You may think that your child is not taking in anything that you are teaching him, but one day he will surprise you and control his anger. Congratulations! Let your child know that you are proud of him.

You are now on your way to helping your child develop self-control. In the first part of the manual, I showed you how to intervene by lowering your child's expectations, by changing the sequence, by using emotional distraction, and by suggesting calming techniques. I also explained what to do when your child is out of control and when to use incentives and consequences. You can use these strategies without involving your child in any charting. In the second part of the manual, I explained how to help your child become more aware of his anger. You also showed him the importance of considering new information, and together you practiced the art of compromise. Sometimes one approach works better than another. See what works for you and your child.

If you get stuck, you may want to consult with a professional in your area. You can use this manual with a professional, who can help point out issues you may overlook because you are so close to the situation. Also, if there are co-occurring conditions, like a mood disorder or oppositional defiant disorder, or if your child has suffered a trauma, it is advisable to consult with a mental health professional because you will need to do more than the exercises in this manual.

The manual is intended to empower you to help your child with anger overload. Be patient. It takes time, usually months to see significant change. You are teaching your child techniques that change his behavior and his brain. Children with anger overload have strong emotional reactions that overwhelm their rational brain. These techniques will help your child's rational brain to gain control. Your child will feel the pride of mastering a tough problem and learn that hard work pays off.

Appendix

Chart 1: Recording angry interactions

Scenario 1: Date________________

Who was the target adult? _________________

What did the child say or do? ____
____

What did the adult say or do?
____
____

What did your child say or do next?
____
____

What did the adult say or do next?
____
____

Anything happen then? ____

What was your child doing in the hour preceding the above interaction?
____

What was the target adult doing in the preceding hour?
____

Scenario 2: Date________________

Who was the target adult? _________________

What did the child say or do? ____
____

What did the adult say or do?
____
____

What did your child say or do next?

____

____

What did the adult say or do next?

____

____

Anything happen then? ____

What was your child doing in the hour preceding the above interaction?

____

What was the target adult doing in the preceding hour?

____

Scenario 3: Date________________

Who was the target adult? ________________

What did the child say or do? ____

____

What did the adult say or do?

____

____

What did your child say or do next?

____

____

What did the adult say or do next?

____

____

Anything happen then? ____

What was your child doing in the hour preceding the above interaction?

____

What was the target adult doing in the preceding hour?

____

Scenario 4: Date________________

Who was the target adult? _______________

What did the child say or do? ____
____

What did the adult say or do?
____
____

What did your child say or do next?
____
____

What did the adult say or do next?
____
____

Anything happen then? ____

What was your child doing in the hour preceding the above interaction?
____

What was the target adult doing in the preceding hour?
____

Scenario 5: Date_______________

Who was the target adult? _______________

What did the child say or do? ____
____

What did the adult say or do?
____
____

What did your child say or do next?
____
____

What did the adult say or do next?
____
____

Anything happen then? ________________________________

What was your child doing in the hour preceding the above interaction?

____

What was the target adult doing in the preceding hour?

____

Scenario 6: Date________________

Who was the target adult? ________________

What did the child say or do? ________________________________

____

What did the adult say or do?

____

____

What did your child say or do next?

____

____

What did the adult say or do next?

____

____

Anything happen then? ________________________________

What was your child doing in the hour preceding the above interaction?

____

What was the target adult doing in the preceding hour?

____

(Feel free to make more copies of chart #1, or any of the charts that follow.)

Chart 3: For each situation, what is my strategy?

I. One situation where there has been anger overload in the last two weeks:

____

____

Prevention:

How could I prepare my child in advance? ____________________________________

Could I alter the routine and avoid the trigger?

____

Is my child insecure about something and does that underlie these outbursts?

____

Early anger phase:

Possible emotional distractions:

____

Possible calming strategies: ____

Overload phase:

Do I ignore or restrain? ______________

Will I use a consequence (afterwards) and what will it be?

____

Will I use an incentive if there are fewer outbursts? ___________________________

II. Another situation where there has been anger overload in the last two weeks:

____

____

Prevention:

How could I prepare my child in advance? ____________________________________

Could I alter the routine and avoid the trigger?

____

Is my child insecure about something and does that underlie these outbursts?

____

Early anger phase.

Possible emotional distractions:

____

Possible calming strategies: _______________________________________

Overload phase:

Do I ignore or restrain? __________________

Will I use a consequence (afterwards) and what will it be?

____

Will I use an incentive if there are fewer outbursts? ________________________

Note: After a month, think about which strategies are working and which are not. Change or eliminate those strategies that have had no effect.

Chart 5: Level of anger and bodily sensations

Situation 1: Who got angry? ______________________________

What was the sequence of his (or her) angry statements or behaviors?

a)____ Level______

b)____ Level______

c)____ Level______

Any bodily sensations, and if so, when did they start? _________________________________

Looking back, what was the trigger? ____

Situation 2: Who got angry? ___________________

What was the sequence of his (or her) angry statements or behaviors?

a)____ Level ______

b)____ Level ______

c)____ Level ______

Any bodily sensations, and if so, when did they start? ________________________________

Looking back, what was the trigger? ____

Situation 3: Who got angry? ______________________________

What was the sequence of his (or her) angry statements or behaviors?

a)____ Level______

b)____ Level______

c)____ Level_______

Any bodily sensations, and if so, when did they start? _________________________________

Looking back, what was the trigger? ____

Situation 4: Who got angry? ____________________

What was the sequence of his (or her) angry statements or behaviors?

a)____ Level ______

b)____ Level ______

c)____ Level ______

Any bodily sensations, and if so, when did they start? ___________________________________

Looking back, what was the trigger? ____

Situation 5: Who got angry? ________________________________

What was the sequence of his (or her) angry statements or behaviors?

a)____ Level______

b)____ Level______

c)____ Level_______

Any bodily sensations, and if so, when did they start? ____________________________________

Looking back, what was the trigger? ____

Situation 6: Who got angry? ____________________

What was the sequence of his (or her) angry statements or behaviors?

a)____ Level ______

b)____ Level ______

c)____ Level ______

Any bodily sensations, and if so, when did they start? ___________________________________

Looking back, what was the trigger? ____

Chart 7: How new information affects anger in your family

Situation 1: ______________________________

Who was the target of your child's anger? ______________________________

What did your child say or do? ______________________________

What did your child find out (or realize) later? ______________________________

How did your child feel then? ______________________________

Situation 2: ______________________________

Who was the target of your child's anger? ______________________________

What did your child say or do? ______________________________

What did your child find out (or realize) later? ______________________________

How did your child feel then? ______________________________

Situation 3: When you (one of the parents) got angry: ______________________________

Who was the target of your anger? ______________________________

What did you say or do? ______________________________

What did you find out (realize) later? ______________________________

How did you feel then? ______________________________

Chart 8: Using catch phrases

Situation 1: Who got angry with whom? ______________________________

What did the person who got angry say or do? ____________________________

Who mentioned a catch phrase and what was it? ____________________________________

What did the person who got angry say or do next?_________________________

Looking back now, what was the trigger?

____

Looking back now, what was another way of looking at the situation?

____

Situation 2: Who got angry with whom? ___________________

What did the person who got angry say or do? _____________________________

Who mentioned a catch phrase and what was it? __________________________________

What did the person who got angry say or do next?__________________________

Looking back now, what was the trigger? ____

Looking back now, what was another way of looking at the situation?

____

Situation 3: Who got angry with whom? ___________________

What did the person who got angry say or do? _____________________________

Who mentioned a catch phrase and what was it? __________________________________

What did the person who got angry say or do next?__________________________

Looking back now, what was the trigger? ____

Looking back now, what was another way of looking at the situation?

____

Situation 4: Who got angry with whom? ______________________________

What did the person who got angry say or do? ____________________________

Who mentioned a catch phrase and what was it? ______________________________

What did the person who got angry say or do next?__________________________

Looking back, what was the trigger? ____

Looking back, what was another way of looking at the situation?

____

Situation 5: Who got angry with whom? ___________________

What did the person who got angry say or do? _____________________________

Who mentioned a catch phrase and what was it? _____________________________

What did the person who got angry say or do next?__________________________

Looking back, what was the trigger? ____________________________________

Looking back, what was another way of looking at the situation?

____

Situation 6: Who got angry with whom? ___________________

What did the person who got angry say or do? _____________________________

Who mentioned a catch phrase and what was it? _____________________________

What did the person who got angry say or do next?__________________________

Looking back, what was the trigger? ____________________________________

Looking back, what was another way of looking at the situation?

____

49817096R00036

Made in the USA
Lexington, KY
21 February 2016